DEAR

MIDNIGHT

zack grey

for those who
are still learning
to love the dark

contents:

dear midnight,

i haven't always loved you like i should.

it is easy to be persuaded by the way the
sun shines as she greets me, but true warmth
is in the way you wrap my body in soft
blankets of black velvet sky when no one
else is around to ease my troubled mind.

the sun will always
rise & set,

but at the end of every day there is darkness.

your love is not always kind,
but it is honest,
and i will learn to thrive in it
just as i do in the light.

sunrise

zack grey

"ciao," she said,
and i fell in love
with the idea of
a girl who cannot
decide between
'hello' and 'goodbye'.

you smile like
helium
and i
float.

you laugh like you
don't care who's watching.
it's in moments like these
that my preoccupied heart
begins to loosen and
ready itself
to dive into you.

FALLING

INTO YOU

i look at you
and think of
how perfectly
the curve of
your hips
would fit the
palm of my
hand and
i can't understand
why you have to be
so far away.

zack grey

your dove laugh

flies free

and i

know that

i am meant to

fly

with you

with you

with you.

my heart rises like
the sun

when it's set
on you.

zack grey

you found me   da
                n
                g
                l
                i
                n
                g

in front of you,

a loose thread

looking for someone

to
    p u l l

        it.

and pull you did

around & around & · never ending ·

zack grey

what i'm trying to say is

you

me.

i love you frantically
socks charging up
static electricity
as i pace the room
overthinking every
possibility
i want you to
send a shock
through my system
every time i say
am i alive?
i want you
to touch me
zap
like the
sistine chapel
fingers creating
a new kind of life
together
balloon
stuck to my head
maybe i look silly
but god this
feels great

i love you frantically
fishing rod
reel you in
hope the line doesn't
break
hope the perfect
catch
takes the bait
hope i have the
patience
to wait

i love you frantically.
spilling old goodbyes
on your shirt
god they hurt
but maybe this can
work.

i love you frantically.
can we practice
saying hello
until my heart beats
96 times per minute

hello hello hello
hello hello
hello

there it is.

hi.

i love you.

zack grey

your hands
worrying
the out of line
curvature
of my spine

my mouth at
the nape of your
neck

toes, tangled.

a moment
that will
outlive
us

butterflies kissed
the sun & you
kissed me the same way:

like a dream you
never want to
wake up from.

i was watching the sun rise
and you were sleeping
by my side.

i smiled to myself and thought
so this what it feels like
to dream with eyes *wide open.*

zack grey

tonight i
slept without the tv on
because reality is finally
so beautiful
that i am no longer
afraid
of the dreams
that will bloom from my mind
when the world is
silent.

she is layered. i see first her smile; how
cliche, you might say, except you haven't
seen hers. she smiles like a sunflower
reaching for the sky. she smiles like a dodo
bird back from extinction. she smiles like
she just saw the love in my eyes for the first
time. every. single. day.

i peel back what is noticeable at first glance
and find another layer. a sunflower, a bird—
the metaphor is irrelevant. just know that,
like these things, there is more to her than
meets the eye, but only if you open the ears
of your heart. if you listen with your soul. if
you smile with your hands and bleed with
your tears. there is more to her. there is
more,

and more, and more, and more yet because
i am not done— another layer reveals that
she doesn't even belong to this world. yes,
she sees herself as a person, but i have never
met a perfect person. yet she is perfect. if i
understand occam's razor at all, the natural
conclusion is that she is simply not a person.
she is an otherworldly creature and
perfection is within her reach, unlike me.

zack grey

i am not done, nor is she. she has more
layers than i will ever find, but i don't need
to know every inch of her right away.

i love her like i love solving mysteries—
i am content to learn a single new thing each
and every day.

she is many-layered, and in most lifetimes,
beyond my reach. but in this one, nature has
revealed itself to me.

she is a rose, perfect in her anatomy.

zack grey

we woke up
before the sun
to see it rise;

you watched the sky
and i looked at you
the whole time.

zack grey

she had arms like clouds
and eyes that kept saying hello
even when she let go.

zack grey

i cried today
and it was
like the way
the sun showers
its rays
on us all,

tears of joy
for the first time
because i finally
saw

what it means
to experience something
so beautiful
that this vessel
of skin and bone

can no longer
contain
the vast oceans
inside it.

lifetimes ago,
it was you.

it's still
you.

you smelled like lean in closer.
you looked like don't close my eyes.
you moved like just be still.
and i wanted to meet your laugh
in closed quarters
to see if i could feel
the ground rumbling
and the heat of your breath
swaying the hairs of my neck.
i wanted to see you cry
just to find out
if the ocean in your soul
could flow into the smallest parts of me
like rivers in the distance.
i held you close
like feel my heartbeat?
and you smoothed my hair
like it's alright honey.
what i'm saying is,
you loved like
just don't go.
and i listened like
maybe i finally believe.

you taste like regret
and
i **love** how
familiar it is.

sunset

zack grey

my heart was

soar *ing*

faster than my
head could spin,
but these
whirlwinds
always end the same:
with my back on the ground,
hoping
to be picked up
again.

zack grey

i whispered her name
like a dirty
secret.

in my home,
that's all love
ever was.

zack grey

we forgot how to love
today
by worrying about
tomorrow.

zack grey

people like us—

we already knew
the power of words,
but we used them recklessly
anyway.

zack grey

we lost ourselves
in each other
but we still lost
~~ourselves~~.

zack grey

zenith.
then we reached our

a ferris wheel stuck at the top.
calming at first, uneasy after a while,
eventually,
just tired.

i'd still feel your head
resting on my shoulder,
but i'd never believe
it didn't want to be
anywhere else.

up, upupup,

down, but only because
we couldn't be closer.

down, but only because
i am still learning to leave
my baggage at the door,

still learning to slip off my shoes,
to take a seat only when asked,
to say yes, please, that would be lovely,
when you offer me a glass of water.

up, because sometimes i find it
within myself to peel off this toxic
skin that has grown over the surface
and radiate in the positive sense
instead.

up, because you remembered the little
things.
you taught me the importance of
saying i love you even when i don't feel it,
calling back to earlier conversations when
we jinxed each other and realized that's
what love actually is. it's a jinx.

i love you. ha, look. we said it
at the same time.
isn't that cute?

down, downdowndown,
because i'm missing you.

down, because you're missing me too
but we miss each other most
at different times
and they're never in straight lines,
they curve and zig and zag and they go

d
o
w
n

because when you're the only
person i hurt for
you're the only person
i want to hurt more.

these messed up minds.
aren't we blessed?

up and down and ways i haven't thought of
yet because i haven't learned everything—
just what you could teach me.

this was
the topography of us.

"i'm happy," you said.
"without you," i said,
reminding you of
how we used to finish
each other's sentences.

i don't want to to burn it.
we didn't end in a house fire, we ended in a
flood.
we were so full of ourselves, that a cup
could not possibly contain the amount
of pride that we needed to swallow.

i don't want to burn it.
you don't burn love, you fold it up
and carry it in your back pocket
like a favorite letter that you read over and
over, taking it out whenever you forget what
it felt like the first time.

i want to collect love like poetry. like pages
that go together in a book that will always
be right there on the coffee table in my
living room. a book that i can open and
show to guests when they enter my home. a
book full of pages that i can point to and say
yes, i loved like that, once. a book that is not
full, but just beginning.

i don't want to burn love
just because it has passed,
i want to cradle it in my arms like a newborn
child screaming at the top of its lungs
i have entered the world.

she didn't call &
she didn't call &
she didn't call &
eventually, it stopped
hurting,

because when you
learn to expect
the sun to set,
you're no longer
surprised
when it
always does.

zack grey

i was sand
sifting
through your
fingers,

you were the
glass-making
heat of
passion.

we were bottles
broken in bar fights;
pieces shattered
on the floor.

i hope he
knows how
to make a
mosaic;

i'm still waiting for
her artist hands
to wave
hello.

zack grey

i rub sleep from my eyes
stretch my arms out wide
wiggle my toes
greet the sun like
where have you been?
waking up is easier now,
i'm in love again.

WAKING UP

FROM YESTERDAY

i wrapped her up,
tied a bow on it
like a gift
meant for
someone else,

then i looked at you
like the sunlight
i've been missing.

i'm moving on
from yesterday.

zack grey

same hearts
tangled
legs & arms
beginnings with ending
backwards started we

zack grey

you taste ~~like regret~~
~~and~~
~~i love how~~
familiar ~~it is~~.

zack grey

you were the ocean
and i an unsuspecting vessel

loaded with yesterdays that
just wouldn't go overboard.

capsizing

zack grey

i lean in to the
nape of your neck;
you smell like fear.

how beautiful it is to know
that we are afraid of
the very same thing.

love

zack grey

if you are broken
and i am broken
why don't we trade pieces
and make something new?

zack grey

"loving me is
dangerous,"
she says.

"and i like to skydive
without a parachute,"
i tell her.

she traces the scar on my back
with curious fingers like
she's finally found a resting place
for her healing hands.

zack grey

i'd rather fight with you
than smile at her

(i'd do anything
to keep my name
on your lips)

zack grey

i told her what you said—

that i was a hurricane
who could only love
with gale force winds.

she laughed like you used to
when i said something
ridiculous,

and she told me that
the forces of nature
are a magician's best friend.

zack grey

imagine a story
that goes like this:

he held onto her
& he
never let go.

midnight

we are a
generation of
almost lovers,
gazing with
gleaming eyes
at the moon,
knowing she empathizes
with our same hearts
always missing each other
by nothing more
than those few minutes
that separate
darkness
from daylight.

zack grey

i'm still trying to shed myself
of this idea that love
is like a shoe
that was only made
to fit other people.

zack grey

you taste like love
and
i *regret* how
familiar it is.

zack grey

she smiled and my knees buckled.
she said, "i love you" and my
heart burst into flames and
i forgot how to
stop drop and roll.
she said, "i need some time to myself"
and i waited.
she said, "i need some time to myself"
and i waited.
she said, "i need some time to myself"
and i waited,
dangling from her string
like a fly trapped in a spiderweb.
and i forgot for a moment
that i am not anyone's prey.

zack grey

tonight i gazed at the sky
like i always do
and it looked just as beautiful
as it was last night, except
i think i can hear the stars
laughing at me
just like you did when
i told you i loved you
and you didn't say it back.

zack grey

she let me go
like grains of sand
sifting through her
hands: softly and
mindlessly.

i let her go like a
balloon tied too
loosely to my wrist,

which is to say,
not at all,
but i still had to
watch her

f l o a t   a w a y.

zack grey

we were a living story
that has become
nothing more than
a table of contents:

1. how she flirted
and swore that 'hello'
is not a flirty word.

2. how he became her moon
and she was a hurricane
beyond his control.

3. how they wanted the impossible
but she viewed it as a shooting star
wish, and he saw it as a dream
that could come true.

4. how it hurt to love her
without holding her.

5. how 'never' was in her vocabulary
but he didn't even know
the meaning of the word.

zack grey

6. when she left.

7. when she came back.

8. when he left.

9. when he came back.

10. when she left.

11. and stayed gone.

12. and met someone else.

when you said 'goodbye'
i carved l-o-v-e in my skin
just so i would never forget
what it feels like to bleed
your name.

because you were
coursing, coursing, coursing
through my veins
your words
your hands
your mirthful smile—

all
a part of me.

now that you're gone,
everything i hold feels like you.

the key to my car
(just the right shape
to turn it on)

the remote to my television
(i always knew just how
to press your buttons)

these shards of glass
(you always did find
beauty in destruction)

freshly cut roses
(i held too tight;
you cut me open)

my camera
(we were picture perfect
until you zoomed out
like i wasn't worth it)

my morning coffee
(kept me going until
i crashed without you)

this pen this notebook these words
(you're a story worth telling)

the girl i met last night
at the bar
(i was imagining you
the whole time)

myself. together.

it burns.
not the whiskey, or the
gasoline i've doused myself
with— the way she never
looked back. it burns. little
holes spreading across my
lungs. do you think she'd do
it again if she knew i can't
breathe anymore? it burns.
i feed it with oxygen, every time
i check in on how she's been.
it burns like i'm an ant under
a magnifying glass. she smiles
like everything is perfect. i laugh
like it doesn't hurt. i'm lying.
it burns. it burns. it burns.

zack grey

~~and with time, it will heal.~~

time has only taught me
that the wound never closes.
the blood never stops flowing—
a torrent simply becomes a trickle
a trickle becomes a misting

a misting, a single drop.

like water torture, a single
drop
drop
drop

washes away
the mile high barriers
placed in our head.

with time,
it dies.

but death is not always
permanent.

with time,
it haunts.

zack grey

i see your bonfire hands
touch him

my car alarm mind rings
with worry

his smoke eyes
fill your lungs

this celluloid memory
plays movies in my head

i always hated
horror flicks

zack grey

today i
wore the cologne
you bought me,

and everyone said
i smelled like
heaven.

maybe that's
what it is,
the memory of you:

exactly like heaven,
just another place
i'm not allowed into.

zack grey

i have washed this
stained shirt
over and over;

stained with coffee,
stained with you.

it's been forever now
and the coffee
has washed out

but your scent still
lingers.

zack grey

& she breathes.
do you feel that?

when it's cold outside
she still exhales frost.

rain still runs down her skin,
tiny droplets of yesterday.

the moon still shines
light on her face

even though she
changed his name.

listen.
do you hear that?

it's the sound of
laughter.

she still lives in you,
but you're dead to her.

after you left, love became a leaky roof.

drip,
drip,
dripping

slowly but surely. love became something
that needed to be contained; a bucket, filled
and drained every once in a while.

without you, love became a late october
evening when i was still wearing summer
clothes. bearable, most nights. but some
nights i felt so damn cold all i did was hug
myself to keep warm, wishing it was you
instead.

you see, love didn't go away just
because you did. love stays, even when
people don't.

if you came back right now and tried to fix
it all, love would probably make me try to
forgive you, until the next time. not that i'd
want to— my human says no. says that you
are the reason it hurts so much. says that you
can't be trusted with
something as fragile as a heart when you
can't even look at windows without
breaking them.

i have a million more words for you, but
most of them look like

youleftyouleftyouleft

youhurtmeyouhurtmeyouhurtme

stayawaystayawaystayaway

and after a while they all begin to look the
same. say the same things. taste the same
way.

loving you even after you stopped loving me
is drinking milk even after it's gone sour.

if i know you, you're lying in bed right now
thinking of me. smiling because you're so
satisfied with the way hearts fall into your
hands. laughing because you can feel the
hurt transcending the distance and begging
you to give it shelter. crying because you
know eventually i'll move on and you'll still
be sticking pins in dolls, wondering why it
doesn't work anymore.

i'll admit, i'm still thinking of you, but my
therapist says that if you keep thinking of
something horrible for long enough that,
eventually, it won't seem so bad anymore. so
i'm thinking about the rest of my life
without you.

i see myself smiling, laughing, crying.
there's a girl beside me every step of the
way, doing the same. and she looks
nothing like you.

zack grey

i passed someone
on the street today

who looked nothing
like you.

i think i'm
falling in love.

zack grey

she looks at me with
mist in her eyes
and i can see the
battle she's already
lost in her mind.

for the first time,
we're both playing
our roles just right.

she's vulnerable when she
never has been,
and i'm strong when
i'm usually weak.

"i just want back
what's mine,"
she says,
"your heart."

and i smile as i
walk away because
now she knows
what it's like to
spill her guts
on the floor
and have to
clean them up
all by herself.

zack grey

i held her close
last night
and you floated
above us like

*i'm holding someone else too
don't you wish it was you?*

and i looked into her
dark black ocean eyes,
not wanting to drown in
anything else

but you floated above us
laughing like

*i am alive in
everything you touch*

*if she warms you up
i will be the cool breeze
tickling your neck*

if she smiles at you
i will jump through her teeth
and remind you of
how quickly i let you go

how she lit her candle
and brought you home

but there was still a hurricane
raging inside of you
that she could not contain

thrash thrash
thrash against the binds
i tied you with
but you cannot break them
and she doesn't know
a spell more powerful
than my lies.

zack grey

when the world has finally
decided it's okay to dream
and my mind is refusing
to take a break,

i walk outside into the
cold cold night
and look at the sky to find
someone as restless as me.

a star is shooting and
for the first time,
i make a wish:
please please be quiet.

zack grey

when it's all said and done,
you will destroy me
and i'll ask for more.